Happy Thanksgiving
We are thankful
for you!

Dave & Jes

5 LIES THAT WILL RUIN YOUR REAL ESTATE CAREER

AND THE TRUTH THAT CAN MAKE YOU WEALTHY

5 LIES THAT
WILL RUIN YOUR REAL ESTATE CAREER

AND THE TRUTH THAT CAN MAKE YOU WEALTHY

Todd Tramonte

Best Selling Author of

<u>The New Rise in Real Estate</u> and

<u>Live Free – The Art of the 2 Year Flip</u>

Founder and Broker, Market Experts Realty & The Todd Tramonte Home Selling Team

Founder and President, Real Estate Growth Systems

Copyright © 2017 by Todd Tramonte
ISBN-13: 978-1500258955 *ToddTramonte.com*

Printed in the United States of America. All rights reserved. No part of this publication may be reproduced, stored in a retrieval system, or transmitted in any form or by any means—electronically, mechanically, photocopying, recording, or any other— except for brief quotations in printed reviews, without the prior permission of the publisher.

Every effort has been made to make this book as complete and accurate as possible. This text should be used only as a general guide and not as the ultimate reference source. This publication is sold with the understanding that neither the author nor the publisher is rendering legal, financial, investment or other professional advice or services. Questions relevant to those areas should be addressed to competent members of those professions.

The recommendations in this publication are based on the author's experience and research, believed to be reliable and accurate, but not infallible. The examples presented in this publication have been chosen solely to demonstrate given points. The reader should conduct a thorough investigation of their applicability to the reader's individual circumstances.

The purpose of this publication is to educate and entertain. The author and/or publisher shall have neither liability nor responsibility to any person or entity with respect to any loss or damage caused, or alleged to be caused, directly or indirectly by the information contained in this book.

To the dream you had when you first thought about a career in real estate. To the vision you have of success, freedom, excitement, meaningful value and a life well lived.

To my family and my friends who all give me the fire in my gut to get up every day, head out into the world and share my God-given gifts full out. You make me better.

To my team who make ideas like this book and others happen. Your gifts, tolerations and commitment allow us all to be right where God wants us, serving others.

This is a great read and I plan to use with new recruits to my team. Love the information that Todd imparts here, and I encourage every broker to share this with their agents.
Jeff Quintin
The Quintin Group, Broker

Most agents get into the business because of one of these 5 Lies, often because we want time and financial freedom. We usually end up with time freedom and no financial freedom to enjoy it. If we want Exponential Freedom in our business, this book will set us free from lies we've been told and put us on the path to building a true business, not a part time career.
Matt Johnson
Founder of Pursuing Results & Co-Host of Real Estate Uncensored

In an industry that thrives on empty hype and selfish promotion, Todd cuts through the clutter and breaks down the ugly truth about the lies you've been told about real estate. Building a "real" real estate business is hard, there is no way around that. But if you listen to the simple truths in this book, you will be that much farther ahead of the game. There is no coincidence that Todd has built a multi-million-dollar real estate business, he walks the walk in both his personal life and as a servant leader in his businesses. Take notice of Todd, he is the real deal ... and he is preaching what the real estate industry needs right now...truth!
Lars Hedenborg
CEO, High Performance Real Estate Advisors

I wish this book would have been available when I started in real estate! I learned these things the hard way after

years of trial and error. Great information, easy read!
Kari Cross
Owner, The Cross Group

I love how Todd delivers the truth in the Real Estate business world. Yes, you can be very successful in Real Estate, but don't buy into the common lies you hear every day. Great stuff.
Nick Kremer
Founder, Driven Leads

This is not a part time job, this is a career. If you want to succeed in it, you need to change your thinking. This is not rocket science, it's real estate. You can do it, but you need to stop lying to yourself. You need to stop focusing on what is not important and focus on getting your career started. Todd nails what I preach to my team and coaching clients. You need to read, re-read, and implement what he talks about in this book. Your career depends on it.
Brett Baker
Owner, Boldly Different

In our age of real estate media overload and cable home improvement shows that sexify easy real estate glory and money with little or no time commitment, Todd provides poignant, potent concrete practices that light the path (and the hard work) of real estate success.
Mark A. Wise
Broker, The Wise Choice

In our age of real estate media overload and cable home improvement shows that sexify easy real estate glory and money with little or no time commitment, Todd provides

poignant, potent concrete practices that light the path (and the hard work) of real estate success.
Mark Martin
President, Real Estate Champions

Todd's new book is packed with a lot of practical help on how to have -a great real estate business. Not only does he address the lies that will hurt your career but gives simple, hopeful and effective ways to combat those lies and implement strategies for success!
Brian Bundy
Owner, Bundy Realty Group

These 5 lies are something I had to discover on my own. I wish I had read this 5 years ago when I started in Real Estate.
Albert Garcia
Realtor / Remax

A lot of real estate agents, new & seasoned, will tell you that working with home buyers is a waste of time, and that finding home "sellers" is the only way to sustain a real estate business... I disagree completely... If you have a convenient home search website (Real Geeks, etc.) with an integrated CRM, and you treat your clients like GOLD, you will not only make them raving fans, but you will also make them raving referral clients for the rest of your career. AND by the way, home buyers will most likely become home sellers within 8 years on average.

Give your customers an unforgettable experience... create a system to follow up with them regularly... and you will have built a business that will sustain itself!
Jake M. Bestic, PA
Broker Associate, Realtor
Coldwell Banker Vanguard Realty

In many respects I absolutely agree with Todd, as only a well-rounded agent or team can produce at a high level, consistently. Agents need to have expertise in marketing, negotiations, client care as well as presentation skills. Only then will they be successful in any market. Being a effective real estate agent is not the number of transactions or amount of money one makes, but the positive impact one has on the lives of every client. Regarding the broker model and the splits that are out there, I have a different take. I fully agree, that a broker offering training and hand holding should get compensated for exactly that. An experienced agent, knowing the market, constantly improving his/her skills, adapting to changes, and hiring the right support, can be very rewarding for a broker as well, especially, when it comes to planning and security of the business.
Frank Heitzer
REmax, Real Estate Expert

So many people get into the business 'to make big money and have flexible, free time", this simply isn't reality. Todd lays out the truth required to be a successful agent.
Deb Espinoza
Broker Associate, REALTOR, National Association of Expert Advisors; GRI, SRS, ABR, SFR, CNE

Kudos to Todd for pointedly telling it like it is. This book will help agents set appropriate goals and expectations as they work for their next breakthrough toward real estate success.

David Brownell
Broker/Realtor since 1995
Keller Williams Realty

The simple breakdown of the 5 lies certainly make their point! I agree with the information provided and have been finding quite a bit of fluff out there in my Real Estate career thus far. The ability to sift through the nonsense will go much further for the beginning agent than anything a "coach" can sell you or tell you! With so much information out there on how to be successful in Real Estate, sometimes you just need to take a step back and go with the basics. Paralysis by Analysis is a real thing, and certainly holds true in Real Estate. There is a ton of truth in the 5 Lies presented here!

Robert Cleaver, P.A.
Realty Experts of Florida

I sincerely appreciate this book. I have read through it several times. I wanted to share that this was thought provoking. I have prided myself in being that agent in the 5th Lie and that one really hit me hard. In addition, the 1st Lie hit close to home as well. This book will help me become a better business person.

Christopher P. Cervantez
KALEO Real Estate Company
Real Estate Professional

Contents

Foreword: Jeff Manson	17
Introduction Real Estate Sex Appeal	19
Expert Interview: Frank Klesitz	22
Part One: 5 Lies	27
The 1st Lie	29
Expert Interview: Lori Ballen	34
The 2nd Lie	37
Expert Interview: Nick Kremer	41
The 3rd Lie	43
Expert Interview: Brett Baker	49
The 4th Lie	53
Expert Interview: Jason Simard	59
The 5th Lie	61
Expert Interview: Mike Stadola	65
Part Two: The Truth	69
The Simple Truth	71
Expert Interview: Blaise Timco	96
The Complex Truth	99
Expert Interview: Mike Bell	105
An Amazing **FREE** Offer for You!	107

Appendix: Feedback from "Real" Estate Agents 109

Notes: 119

Foreword

I own a very productive real estate brokerage in Hawaii. I also own a rapidly growing online real estate lead generation and website platform. I work constantly day and night because I love it and because I'm the father of 10 children! I'm an extremely busy person and I don't have a lot of time for distortions of the truth or so-called opportunities that over promise and under deliver. I'm a fan of being a straight shooter, cutting to the chase and honestly, keeping it real.

I met Todd Tramonte in 2011. He was an early adopter of our IDX lead capture website platform. He has been an excellent client and advocate for our technology. His tenure as a user of our product speaks volumes about our commitment to deliver world class value. This is where Todd and I became friends. Over discussions about delivering way above and beyond what a client expects, we've come to a mutual respect and a legitimate friendship.

Todd has set himself and his business apart by an all-out commitment to his faith, his family and to delivering an unparalleled value to his clients. He also has a giant passion to share with others. I've appreciated Todd's frequent feedback about our product and his willingness to share what is working in his business with all Real Geeks customers and me. Many of those users have built businesses off Todd's systems and suggestions.

In the absence of professionals and leaders like Todd Tramonte, many new and experienced agents would pursue and foolishly maintain a course towards a traditional real estate business built on the so called "conventional wisdom." Unfortunately for thousands upon thousands of agents, the accepted truth about the residential real estate industry is not true at all. I tore through the book you're about to read twice in one weekend and was in total agreement with the honesty that Todd shares here.

Real estate is a business and it involves real work. Agents must approach their careers as business owners. Todd cuts through the garbage that is often sold to prospective and new agents and then sadly perpetuated for struggling agents for entire careers. He exposes the myths around discipline and structure as an agent. He tells us the truth about lead sources and the part time approach. Todd is honest about real estate not being a career option for everyone and he hits a home run with his ideas about skill, marketing and sales.

Read this book. Buy copies for friends who are in the business or getting into the business, work hard, and keep it real!

Jeff Manson
Founder,
Real Geeks

Introduction
Real Estate Sex Appeal

Much like the air brushed images of models on the front covers of magazines all over the world, the pictures that many have, and are presented with, of the residential real estate industry are far, far from the truth. Sadly, not all magazine subscribers are in on the gig and many don't know how far from reality those images really are.

In the same way many real estate professionals, and not just the new ones, have been presented with terribly inaccurate ideas of how success is earned in our world. Many agents have been operating based on this false information for years and it continues to be fed to them by a broken industry filled with many broken business models.

When I was in junior high, another kid at football practice offered me a ridiculous tip about girls. He said, "be careful with girls, some of them seem good from far, but are far from good."

While that advice turned out to be not only offensive but completely worthless regarding women, it just so happens to apply to many of the traditional ideas about success as a real estate agent. The stereotypical conversation includes a lot of talk about money and tons of time off when the reality is a career with great potential for income and flexibility with time resulting from quite a bit of hard work.

Many of the ideas that are perpetuated about making money, getting clients, closing sales, marketing, client care, broker agent relationships and the technical expertise required to succeed sound good from far away, but when looked at closely and tested, turn out to be quite far from the good ideas they originally represented.

You, like me, want a career that provides in many different ways. You may have been drawn to real estate because of what you were told about the potential and opportunity one can capitalize on as a real estate agent, broker, franchise owner or team leader. If you really are like me, you quickly discovered that the real world and the real road to success are a whole different ball game than what is advertised.

In the chapters that follow, I've given my thoughts, formulated from many years of hard earned lessons about how to do things wrong and about how to do some things right. I've had the good fortune to learn consistently and study my craft. I've been in several different business models as an investor, agent, team leader, franchise owner and independent brokerage owner.

There are no gimmicks here. Just good solid information you can use to initiate some decision making about where your career is headed. I hope this helps. I'm quite confident it will.

Recommendation:

Stay away from the fantasy land of reality TV Shows about zillion dollar homes and cocktail party negotiations. Success happens through daily commitment and consistently working proven systems.

BONUS

View a daily activity tracker/plan at:
5LiesBook.com/Resources

Big 6 / Goal Sheet

Be Proactive today... not reactive!

Prioritize important items over "urgent" items.

What do you NEED to do TODAY to get what you WANT?

1. _____ A
2. _____ B
3. _____ C
4. _____
5. _____
6. _____

____ calls made ____ contacts ____ appts set ____ executed ____ f2f appts ____

Check one box per outbound call: √ = Call / X = Contact / * = Appointment

Expert Interview: Frank Klesitz

CEO & Co-Founder – Vyral Marketing

Frank Klesitz, is the CEO and Co-Founder of Vyral Marketing, a done-for-you video marketing company in Omaha, NE. The company provides helps professionals (Real Estate, Finance, Chiropractic, and other related fields) stay in better touch with their customer database with video.

1. What do you think is the biggest lie about real estate?

By far the biggest lie is that you must go out and "sell your soul" to interrupt people all day to build your business. That includes cold calling, convincing strangers to hire you, and pounding the phones like a robot to get clients. It's a lie, too, that you must beat up your friends and family for business. The perception that you "have to be a pest" for people to remember you and give you referrals is false. The whole real estate industry tries to paint that as a positive by creating a guilt-based sales culture where you receive recognition to cold call and bug your friends and family. The key, rather, is to get permission *first* to stay in touch with homeowners by offering them a free subscription to your newsletter or to attend your free community event(s). Then, nurture those people into warm conversations with helpful, educational, and even entertaining material that's of value to them.

2. What is the best advice you have about building a real estate career?

Don't lead with your primary offer to a cold market. Your primary offer is to hire you to buy or sell a house. Not everyone is interested in that, and it's presumptive to ask people to hire you the very first time you meet them. Rather, lead with a secondary offer. A great secondary offer is a free subscription to your community real estate newsletter or to attend one of your upcoming community events. It's so much easier to pick a high-turn over farm of let's say 5,000 homes where 6% sell a year. There are 300 deals in that list. All you need to do is buy the contact information of all the homeowners and start talking to them. First, to start the relationship, offer them an item of value (free newsletter subscription or ticket to an event) and ask permission to stay in touch. However, before you even do that, I suggest you reconnect with all the people in your current database first. These are your past clients, sphere, and any good leads you've been working. Make sure you stay in touch with them *before* you work on establishing yourself in a new market. The return on investment is better.

3. What is the best long-term truth you have learned?

You must understand a professional service is different than a business. There are different rules when it comes to selling the intangible. Professional services are marketed differently. Does your lawyer or doctor offer a special discount on their rate? No. The profit for any professional service is all in the *relationship*. It's how you make people feel – people will pay more for a feeling than anything else. Your customer must *feel* you are the best person to guide and protect them in a transaction. Everything you do must advance your position as the pre-eminent expert in your chosen niche.

4. How do you serve agents?

We'll interview you on a HD webcam to create helpful Q&A videos to send out to your database, so people call you to list their home. You can get a copy of the video marketing plan we recommend at www.getvyral.com.

Final Thoughts:

Make sure you always reinvest 10% of what you earn in commissions into getting more business. Certainly, no less, and rarely more. If you earn $10,000 a month in commissions on average, your marketing budget is $1,000 a month. Use that money to first do everything you can to stay in great touch with your database, then as your budget grows, use the additional money to add value and to get in front of homeowners in high turn-over neighborhoods consistently.

PART ONE: 5 LIES

5 Lies That Will Ruin Your Real Estate Career.

The 1st Lie

You'll have complete flexibility with your time.

For some inexplicable reason, failing real estate agents have been perpetuating this lie for generations. An agent who is terribly underperforming his or her goals, when asked "how is business," will say things like, "businesses is great" or "the market is on fire."

Sadly, this absence of truth extends even to friends and contacts who inquire about getting into the business. You may have been told, "this business offers 100% flexibility with your time" or "the autonomy in real estate allows you to really build the business of your dreams."

This, for nearly every agent, is simply not true.

The truth, however, is not all weeping and gnashing of teeth.

The truth about a successful real estate agent's relationship with his or her time is that it requires a strategic amount of structure. Having this structure intentionally put into place will allow an agent to have true freedom and flexibility with their time. Many agents struggle with this idea for way too long. Waking up at 9:00AM and strolling into the office around 11:00 is not an exercise in an agent's control over their time, it is a display of a lack of commitment and discipline for success.

The ability to take a four-day weekend doesn't come from laziness and dreaming, it comes from a well thought out and often adjusted and refined system for the use of the most limited resource we have. When a sharp top-producing agent safely takes four days away from his or her business, it is because of careful planning and the discipline to handle all time sensitive items in an organized manner. When the essential items are all addressed and accounted for, only then can you have real freedom with your remaining time.

Picture the following three businesses:

Business 1

Michelle is an individual agent who sells 20 homes each year in her area's average price point. She makes a decent living and likes what she does. She has one transaction pending and is working with a buyer and a seller currently. She wants to go to New Orleans for Mardi Gras for four days. She books a flight and a room and heads out hoping and praying that she doesn't get a call requesting to see houses from her buyer, or buyers needing an amendment for her upcoming closing. And as much as she would love an offer on her listing, she really doesn't want it to come in while she is gone. Instead, she really hopes all of that happens on Tuesday when she gets back so she'll have some idea of how to pay for all that fun in New Orleans.

Business 2

James is a top-producing agent at his office and has an assistant helping him sell 40-50 homes per year. He carries 10 or so listings at a time and works buyers when he must. He is basically always working but is starting to make pretty good money. He wants to go on a four-day trip to play golf in Phoenix with a few buddies. He has his assistant call and send an email to all active clients informing them that he will be out of town from Thursday evening to Monday night and that she will be the primary contact while he is out. He is available for offers and important contract items but will not be available for day-to-day business. She books his flight and room and he heads out hoping to beat his buddies in golf and hoping that only standard stuff happens while he is out, so he can leave his phone in the hotel while he is out. He will probably take it with him anyway. He calls every morning to make sure all his clients are happy.

Business 3

Maria is a team leader of a team of 5 agents and 3 support staff who sell 120-150 homes each year and is growing rapidly. She usually has about 20 listings and her buyer agents sell a few houses each per month. Her support staff handles all the coordination of listings, files and closings. She focuses mostly on business development, marketing and training her team. She planned a four-day trip to San Diego late last year for her and her husband. Her assistant booked the flight and room last year and her team can see on the team calendar that she will be out on a personal trip but won't even miss a beat while she is out. Her staff will handle the daily training meetings, the seller team tracking meeting on Thursday, the morning huddles, the buyer team tracking meeting on Monday, the closing gifts for the two closings on Monday and her agents know who to go to if one of their deals needs help. The team will watch a video that she filmed a while back at their training meeting on Tuesday. She misses the action in the office but is glad to fully unplug for a long weekend.

Which agent has more flexibility with their time? Which has the most structure? Which business do you want?

BONUS

Use a digital calendar like Google. You will be able to view it from a desktop, laptop, tablet, or cell phone. Changes on one device will update to the others.

View an ideal agent schedule:
5LiesBook.com/Resources

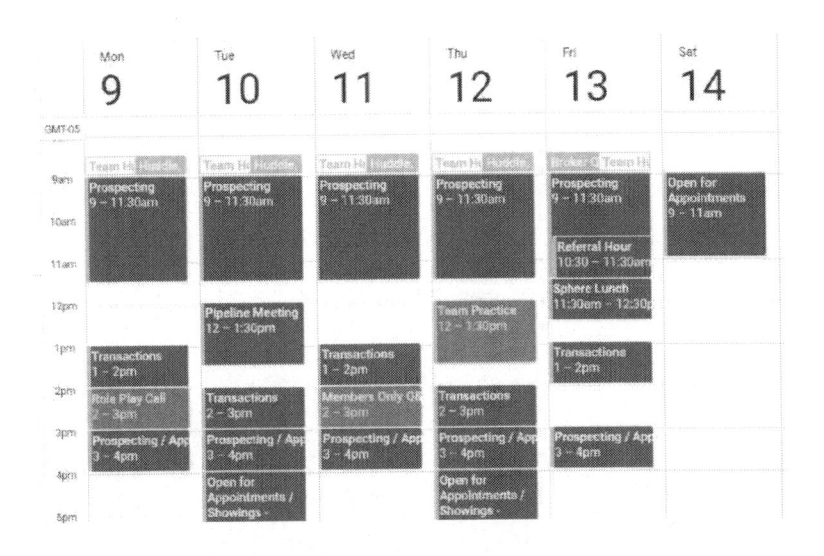

Having this structure in place and put there very intentionally is what will allow an agent to have true freedom and flexibility with time.

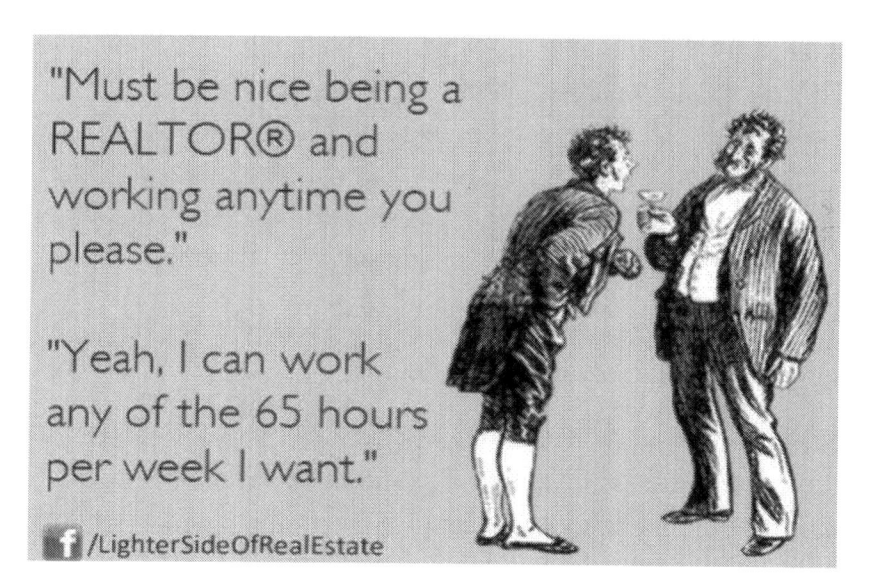

"Must be nice being a REALTOR® and working anytime you please."

"Yeah, I can work any of the 65 hours per week I want."

/LighterSideOfRealEstate

Expert Interview: Lori Ballen

KW Ballen Group & Speaker, Trainer, Author, Coach, Creator of the "Rank Like a Boss" Training Course

Lori Ballen is a Mega Agent with an award-winning real estate team in Las Vegas called The Ballen Group at Keller Williams Realty Las Vegas. Lori has owned multiple successful businesses based on her marketing strategy which is now called "The Ballen Method." She travels and trains other business professionals on her methods.

1. What do you think is the biggest lie you hear or see shared with new agents about real estate?

There is a perception that if new agents have a certain personality type they will be great at real estate, if they are good with people they will be successful at real estate. It isn't just about being a "people person" it is about lead generation. There is a lot of untold information about real estate. There is a skill set that people don't see – the other side - it is taxes, profit & loss as well as lead generation.

2. What is the best advice you have hear about building a real estate career?

No matter what, take massive action. Whatever you do to generate leads, go BIG! People spend a lot of time learning to be an agent instead of being an agent. Half the battle is showing up.

3. What is the best long-term truth you have learned?

Tracking numbers, knowing how you make money is probably the best long-term strategy, as well as know your model. The other long-term advice would be don't let your ego drive your business. It is easy to fall for the shiny object. Newer agents getting started want to be number one in a certain category they go in all different directions and they don't know their numbers because they haven't managed their business. They let their ego drive versus letting the numbers drive their business.

4. How do you serve agents?

My number one way I guide people is really helping them with lead generation efforts and putting a focus on it. I do have services where we build lead generation websites, and content marketing. How I best help is to empower people to do lead generation. We can do it for them, but I want to show them that they need to own their own platform and know how to do lead generation at an expert level. Teaching is my passion.

Final Thoughts:

Spend more time working on yourself than focusing on what other people are doing. Focus on your own skill set. Don't get distracted and start picking up every shiny object just because someone else looks successful doing it. We see these mega producers and people want to emulate them. Really dig into that and find out what the real model is. Get up close, poke holes in it and see if it is bona fide before you take it on for yourself. There are a lot of good models in our business we just need to be careful before we go all in.

The 2ND Lie

You'll be successful if you just work your sphere of influence.

Your sphere or circle of influence, meaning the folks you have some level of influence with, is a tremendously powerful asset. Asset is the deliberate word choice there and viewing your relationships this way does not make you a greedy jerk who doesn't value human relationships and people. It does however make you a smart businessperson. The bologna lies in believing that you can enter the business and rely solely on these relationships to provide a full-time income for you.

Situations do occur where people achieve that feat, but they are rarer than most brokers would ever care to admit. Very few of us have such a large, responsive and loyal group of close friends that the law of averages would still produce a significant number of automatic transactions each month or year. If you are happy with six sales per year, this is a great method for achieving real estate happiness. For the rest of us, working a sphere of influence is an absolute must as part of a broader strategy of lead generation, cultivation, conversion and long-term nurturing.

For those that long for a 100% referral business, there are even risks to the stability of this kind of business. I wouldn't wish it on my worst enemy, but I have seen people who have built decent sized businesses around a referral only strategy, lose massive portions of their business and annual income to a single event like a divorce, poor career choice or shift in the market.

A smart and successful real estate agent / business owner will have a much more developed approach that diversifies marketing across new business, existing clients, past clients, advocates and even sub-divides those segments as it makes sense to provide value to each group of clients and prospective clients. This might include online, radio, direct mail, networking, newsletters, blogging, social media, lunches, coffee appointments, personal visits, phone calls, automated drip campaigns, emails, text messages and on and on.

The absolute worst and most dangerous thing that can happen to a newer agent is to get a few or even just one large referral transaction early on. The activity and income generated by such a fortuitous event can blind a new agent from the necessary learning and habit building that needs to happen to lay the groundwork for long-term success. A newer agent would be wise to aim for three to five sources of business and to initially focus on buyers only, or possibly sellers only if there is a clear understanding of the different sides of the business.

A new buyer agent might choose to pursue buyer prospects from online MLS-based lead capture web sites, open houses, daily calls to his/her sphere of influence and some inexpensive direct response mailings.

A smart listing agent getting ramped up would be ahead of the curve if he/she set a goal of one new seller client a month from each of three areas. They might be expired sellers, For Sale By Owner sellers and sphere of influence.

If, however you have a wealthy, well-connected family who believes in handing you a future with little to no hard work invested on the front end (there is hard work required either way) then you can laugh off everything you just read and honor that generous head start by delivering world class service to all those referred to you. Your situation is quite rare.

For the rest of us, solely looking to your personal contacts for 100% of our business is darn near real estate career suicide.

Recommendation:

Start organizing all your personal contacts. Use Microsoft excel or some type of electronic database to start. List the name, phone number, email and a physical address for each person. After you have a complete list, segment it into proven supporters, potential supporters, and remaining contacts. Delete anyone you would never want to do business with.

BONUS

For a helpful tool to move through this process, visit: 5LiesBook.com/Resources

> *...working a sphere of influence is an absolute must as part of a broader strategy of lead generation, cultivation, conversion and long-term nurturing.*

Expert Interview: Nick Kremer

Founder of Driven Leads

Driven Leads is a leader in Online Lead Generation for Real Estate & Mortgage Brokers throughout the country. Nick had a background in Internet Marketing when he had a real estate friend that needed help. The rest is history....

1. What do you think is the biggest lie you hear or see shared with new agents about real estate?

The biggest thing I see and hammer people on is the fact that they are a small business owner. They want to act like an employee. You need to ultimately generate your own business and control your own destiny. The start of your business is very different from "I started my job at xyz..."

2. What is the best advice you have about building a real estate career?

Start with the least expensive stuff – sphere of influence. There are tons of ways to spend your money to try and promote your business. People want to commit a big budget before they know if that's really what they want to do or if they know how to go that route.

3. What is the best long-term truth you have learned?

Never be satisfied. Never close your mind off to learning new things. Learn something new every year. Successful people are the ones that learn to adapt to changing surroundings. The agents/brokers that make changes and keep improving are the most effective. Don't get lazy!

4. How do you serve agents?

We learn from each of our 140 plus real estate agent clients to serve all of them in a proven but customizable way to generate high quality opportunities to engage with potential sales and buyers. We can generate traffic to drive your ideal clients. This used to be very, very hard and it is getting easier and easier with the right technology and strategy. We help you hit the target!

Final Thoughts:

Look for a mentor. Not just leads and a playbook. Someone who can give you a road map, goals, a plan and help guide you along the way. You don't need as many leads, but you need a lot of leadership.

THE 3ᴿᴰ LIE

This is a great part-time career.

No.

No, it is not.

I once deliberately started a fight (virtually) on a blog by writing an article called, "If You're Not Full-Time, Quit!"

Now, before I get hate mail, there are a few very rare exceptions, but they are so rare that I won't even mention them here. Full-time is the only way to consistently offer world-class value to clients over the long haul. How many highly successful lawyers, doctors and CPAs do you know who are part-time? Not many. I'm willing to have a few of you upset with me over that statement and likely many others, but there is a right and a wrong way to do things. When you look a client in the eye and tell them that you have their best interest in mind and will do all that you can to achieve their desired result, you have to check that against the time, attention, expertise and other investments required to deliver on that promise. Integrity matters.

Purchasing or selling a home is a huge deal with tremendous and far-reaching impact in the lives of those we represent. It can't be done a few hours each week or even a few days each week. I've seen countless negotiations go very poorly for the client who is represented by an agent who has simply not seen as many contracts, amendments, appraisals, inspections, mortgages, settlement statements and other important documents, processes, situations and problems as the agent on the other side. It almost feels wrong to completely dominate these agents in negotiations over such important issues.

Real estate is a fast-paced industry with ever changing case law, regulations, ethical boundaries and state licensing standards. Staying current is hard enough, much less staying on the cutting edge of innovation and delivery of real long-term value to clients. A full-time focus allows for an adequate amount of time to be allocated for education, practice, innovation, client acquisition, client care, delivery of value, vendor relationships, negotiation, processing and other crucial elements of a healthy and lasting career in real estate.

Real estate is an industry though and not a single job. The industry offers some roles which can be performed part-time and may be done exceptionally well part-time. Many leading agents and teams have dedicated showing agents who work limited hours exclusively showing homes to buyer clients. They do not write offers or negotiate, but they do have direct client contact during the shopping phase of the purchase transaction. Transaction Coordinators are support staff who typically handle the processing of the purchase or sale file from the point an agreement is reached all the way through closing and funding. This role can be less than full-time in certain scenarios and still be a huge value add to clients and top producing agents.

Now, full-time certainly does not mean that an agent must be glued to a chair, which is stuck inside a cubicle all day every weekday with no autonomy with time. Full-time in the wonderful world of real estate can, even to our occasional detriment, look from the outside like part-time. A knowledgeable agent can negotiate a very important deal from a car, a ballpark, a cruise ship or a hunting camp. A full-time agent with a part-time showing assistant could theoretically work from another country for an extended period.

The technological tools that have allowed agents to achieve much of this are remarkable, but certainly don't compensate for the expertise, experience and wisdom that come with time invested in mastery.

A note here to ambitious and prospective agents:

Full-time is a funny idea. To do this well, you must view this as a business. Full-time often means 70 hours with skipped meals and missed parties. Once earned, full-time may occasionally mean 3 weeks in the Bahamas. Success still will and always will require hard work.

BONUS

For 5 Levels of Commitment Questionnaire, visit: 5LiesBook.com/Resources

A full-time focus allows for an adequate amount of time to be allocated for education, practice, innovation, client acquisition, client care, delivery of value, vendor relationships, negotiation, processing and other crucial elements of a healthy and lasting career in real estate.

YOU GOT CALLED IN ON YOUR DAY OFF?

I REMEMBER HAVING DAYS OFF BEFORE I BECAME A REALTOR

Expert Interview: Brett Baker

CEO & Founder – Boldly Different

Brett Baker is a Real Estate Agent and team leader of The Baker Team in Tri-Cities Washington. After leaving a $200,000 a year career as an Air Traffic Controller with the Federal Aviation Administration, Brett used the tools and training he received from the aviation world to form The Baker Team in 2015.

1. What do you think is the biggest lie you hear or see shared with told new agents about real estate?

There are two big lies. The first being you need to have a flood of incoming leads to generate enough business to live on. The cheaper you can get leads, the more you can get which will increase the number of transactions you can do.

The second would be that you need to start a team, because that's the definition of success in real estate.

2. What is the best advice you have about building a real estate career?

Number of leads isn't the issue. Quality of leads is where you need to focus the most of your time. If you spend your time chasing down 1,000's of cheap, low-quality leads, you won't be able to effectively follow up with them through the process and will likely lose out on them when they chose an agent that has the time. Realistically a single agent cannot effectively handle more than 30 leads a month.

Find a way to get 20-30 QUALITY leads a month and focus on conversion.

I strongly advise against starting a team. Don't start a team! I think this is probably one of the boldest and anti-trendy statements that can be made right now. The problem I see is agents that are barely keeping themselves fed are trying to encourage other agents to join their "team." This usually stems from the team leader generating "a lot" of low quality, cheap leads and running out of time to work them. They start feeling over worked and think that the solution is to add more people to the equation. Usually, the team leader is barely closing enough transactions to keep the team alive, and they can't give the guidance needed to get their teammates to close transactions, so the "team" suffers on for a while until it is no longer sustainable.

3. What is the best long-term truth you have learned?

So many agents treat their career in real estate as a job. This isn't a job; this is a small business. There are many ways to approach doing business, but all of them start with a clear focus on the outcome. When I sit down with people to talk about business planning, I want them to see where they want to be in 5, 10, and 15 years. What does that picture look like to them? We start there and work backward until we finally hit what they must do every day to reach their business goals. It all comes down to strategic planning, dedication, and direction. Once you have a clear focus on what you need to do to reach your goals, it all comes down to following that plan.

4. How do you serve agents?

The Baker Team is known for their bold branding and guerrilla style marketing. Our team has quickly become one of the most successful teams in the Washington market garnering national media attention. Brett does consulting and you can reach Brett and his team at 509-822-BOLD or www.BoldlyDifferent.com.

Final Thoughts:

The most effective way to increase your closed transactions without getting overworked is to have a strategic growth plan in place. By having a plan, you will know when to hire your first admin, transaction coordinator, showing agent, buyer's agent, ISA, etc. Before you know it, you'll have a successful team of highly specialized people that work together to create a systematic approach to real estate.

THE 4TH LIE

The bigger the "split" the better the broker.

Broker / Agent commission splits are like asking prices for homes. They don't mean anything until you've done your research. An alarmingly high number of new, experienced and even top producing agents make the ego-driven and foolish mistake of chasing the highest commission splits available in their market place. We've all heard that "1% of something is better than 100% of nothing," and there certainly are opportunities for agents to have 100% commission arrangements with brokers. These are usually such a poor choice for a full-time expert agent that the commission split discussion usually focuses more in the range of 40% - 90% splits for the agent and 10% - 60% splits for the broker.

It is common for a brand-new agent with zero experience to have a 40/60 or 50/50 arrangement with a broker. In most scenarios, if given a truly honest evaluation, these arrangements are overwhelmingly to the financial benefit of the agent. The broker takes on significant risk with an inexperienced agent and should take on a huge educational and training burden as well. A smart agent starting out will seek out real value from his or her broker and focus less on the percentage they earn from each closed transaction. A really, really smart new agent will see the value in experience, training, client acquisition and reputation. They'll soak up as much knowledge as humanly possible and seek to add as much value as humanly possible. This will certainly lead to higher income and additional opportunity.

It is also common for agents to pay fees to their broker. This shocks many beginners and has been long ago accepted as "how the game is played" by veterans. I've always found it interesting that the most successful businesses track, calculate and analyze their costs of acquisition of talent, clients, assets etc. and invest in the long-term success of those relationships. They risk much early to gain much in the long term. By some heinous miracle of oversight, the residential real estate industry has this so fantastically backwards that it hurts everyone involved. Lackadaisical hiring standards fed by low educational requirements lead to the hiring of just about anyone. This leads to unfathomable rates of turnover. In turn, brokerage owners make up for the virtual absence of revenue in the early stages by charging desk fees, royalty fees, processing fees, copier usage fees, technology fees and other vaguely named fees to simply cover the hard-overhead costs of running the business. When you couple this with the urge to give productive agents much higher commission splits, you start to see why most brokerages are not very profitable at all.

Many productive agents practice what I call aimless extortion. As these agents begin to produce at a high level, they start to see the brokerage model and the gaping holes in the very foundation of the business. They then take the position that they are a major influencer of company success and imply that their leaving would be a major hit to the company. This often results in their commission split rising and the brokerage portion falling. An agent who ends up at a 75/25 or 80/20 split is no longer profitable to the broker and becomes a simple marketing story to tell the next rookie who will pay more fees.

There are exceptions of course, but these are the rules. The all-star rookie who pays low fees and sells a ton of houses is a huge profit center to the company. The rare broker who truly invests in his agents gives real value for the fees he charges. The top producing agent who recognizes his or her skills in sales and marketing and chooses not to manage and own a brokerage or team. All parties benefit in these situations. These, however, are the rare scenarios among the more popular broker jumping strategy to grab more commission split on the same small pie of annual commission earned.

I've always had a partnership approach to agent/broker commission splits. The closer we are to a true mutually beneficial relationship, the more likely we are to invest in each other, take risks for each other and support each other. The second a team member might consider that they want a higher split, they have lost sight of our vision to grow together. The moment I am not providing enough value for my team members, we need to talk. If we can't continue on the same page eagerly, they should seek out another work environment.

The successful approach to commission splits and broker agent relationships lies in an agreement that is intended to and delivers on achieving everyone's goals. Agents want to work with great clients, sell homes, earn great incomes, spend time pursuing their out of work passions, lead families and achieve freedom to choose. Brokers want agents who work hard, produce results, grow their business, reflect their company values and stay for a while. An agent who wants to make more money in this environment comes to their broker and says, "How can I get to my goal of $250,000 this year?" They do not say, "Mike, I need an 80/20 split, or I'll have to go down the road to Bob's office."

A sharp team leader or broker responds by saying "What an awesome question, let's start by analyzing your business from last year…"

Together they focus on marketing, conversion, skills, tracking, transaction size, client quality, referral systems and on and on to achieve each of their goals together. They rely on each other's strengths and compensate for each other's weaknesses. They don't have to be best friends, but they need to respect the value each brings to the relationship and make the effort to maintain the relationship over a long period of time.

Now, of course there are exceptions. Some agents are capable of being a broker and simply chose not to carry the responsibility, expense and risk of that role. They are legitimately self-sufficient or close to it. They may also seek those resources outside of their brokerage. These agents may benefit from a very high split scenario and invest in growth and systems on their own.

BONUS

For a reusable template to help evaluate or interview brokers, visit:
5LiesBook.com/Resources

> *A smart agent starting out will seek out real value from his or her broker and focus less on the percentage they earn from each closed transaction.*

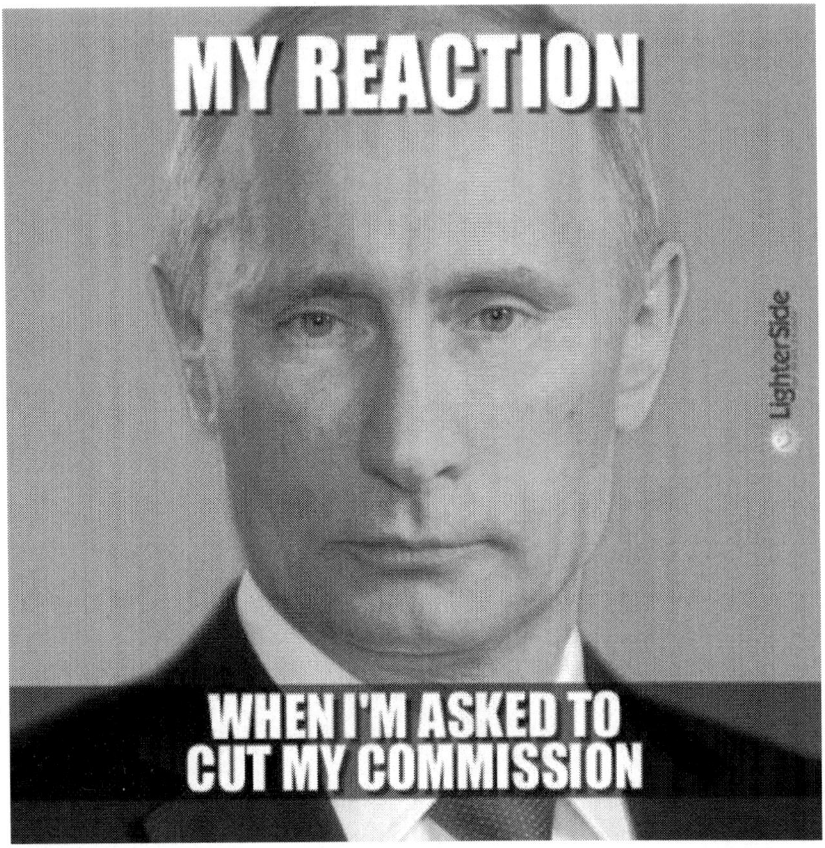
MY REACTION
LighterSide
WHEN I'M ASKED TO
CUT MY COMMISSION

Expert Interview: Jason Simard

Owner, Sims Real Estate Group

Jason Simard maintains a pragmatic, service-driven approach with which he faces every real estate transaction. Jason's passion for real estate started early, as he sold his first investment property at the age of 19. Jason's diverse experience allows him to provide unique insights and exceptional real estate client experiences. He sold 90 homes in his first year of real estate.

1. What do you think is the biggest lie you hear or see shared with new agents about real estate?

Most realtors come into the business thinking about being a top agent. Very few come into the business considering how to build a system to produce consistent income.

2. What is the best advice you have for building a real estate career?

Being a great realtor does not make you a great business owner. Each require different hats. Building an egocentric business that revolves around one person will not take you far. Building a truly client-centric business where everything you and the people within your organization do is catered to the betterment of the consumer – that is where you will find satisfaction and success.

3. What is the best long-term truth you have learned?

Your emotional intelligence is one of the greatest assets you can bring to your real estate career. Knowing your talents and weaknesses will help guide you on where you should focus your time and energy.

4. How do you serve agents?

I serve agents by teaching them how to get leads. I give them the freedom to have success and develop a plan for long term income.

Final Thoughts:
Building systems and processes over time and building a culture of empowered agents takes years, sacrifice, hard work and discipline. Don't fall into the traps many agents do. Shiny object syndrome is a plague in our industry and it stops many agent's dead in their tracks. Analysis paralysis is a silent killer nobody is talking about. Nothing happens unless something happens.

THE 5TH LIE

The best agent always wins.

False.

The best agent sometimes wins, but only when he / she is also the best marketer or when he / she is not in a competitive environment.

Many agents foolishly overlook marketing as a key skill in building a long-term sustainable business with predictable and consistent income. They do this while championing transactional skills. The error is not made in focusing on being a world-class expert in the areas of property analysis, negotiation, contracts, process and transactional details, but in exclusively focusing on these items.

The absolute best real estate agent in the world regarding transactional skill and even experience is limited by his or her ability to attract clients to initially work with and then buyers for their listings and often sellers for their buyers. This doesn't even address the eventual need to attract talented staff. If you can navigate the inner workings of a nine-page state promulgated form a bit better than me, that may make you in some respects a better agent. However, if I can attract and arrange meetings with significantly more prospective clients, I'm going to have significantly more clients with whom to work state promulgated contracts. I'm going to have more clients. I'm going to sell more homes and have more past clients to repeat and refer business. I'm going to tell their stories of success more creatively, effectively and profitably than you.

If your transactional skills allow you to maneuver through the listing process more efficiently and more traditionally, you may be a better agent in some respects. If, however, I am more skilled and effective at presenting the home to attract higher priced offers and can do so quickly with elements of urgency, scarcity and emotional need, I win.

In markets with extremely high housing inventory, my skillset to position my sellers' homes as one-of-a-kind opportunities is a more valuable skillset and will bring my clients and I more success. In markets with extremely low housing inventory, my ability to find my buyers off-market homes, coming soon homes and under radar homes at fair prices will bring my clients and my company more success.

But what if I can do both at an expert level?

The real success is not in over-valuing transactional skill or in hyper-focusing on marketing ability, but in an all-out assault on the traditional model with an extreme dedication to specialized knowledge and sharpened ability in both areas as well as others. The team approach does this well and agents who seek to constantly grow and improve find success more quickly with this approach.

The agent or team who has a world-class transactional process fed by one or more world-class marketing campaigns, followed by a world-class sales process, then followed by a world-class long-term client care process is a winner time and time again.

BONUS

For agent marketing opportunities, visit:
5LiesBook.com/Resources

> *The best agent sometimes wins, but only when he / she is also the best marketer or when he / she is not in a competitive environment.*

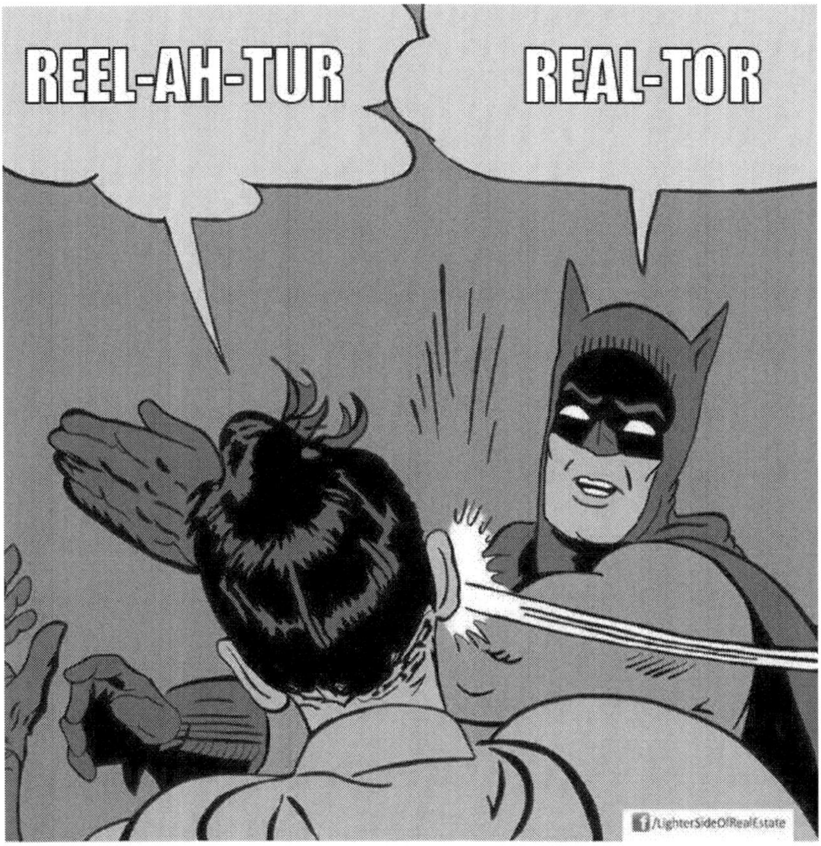
REEL-AH-TUR
REAL-TOR
/LighterSideOfRealEstate

Expert Interview: Mike Stadola

Marketing Strategist

Former Multimillion dollar real estate agent/broker/owner, and Marketing Director for Glazer Kennedy Insider Circle. Current marketing strategist at Powerful Professionals and 10,000 Facebook Fans for Real Estate Agents.

1. What do you think is the biggest lie you hear or see shared with new agents about real estate?

If you tell people you are in real estate and get your name out there you will get enough business. People think that by getting exposure or fame or recognition you will get business. You won't.

2. What is the best advice you have for building a real estate career?

Offer value and collect information. When you build relationships make sure you are following up. Make sure you are adding value to them and offering something to them instead of just asking for business. Always capture the information!!!! Do a monthly mailed follow up to build deeper relationships.

3. What is the best long-term truth you have learned?

Be intentional. You must have a planned outcome. You can't just expect to try something as a one off and expect success. Your long-term plan must be a strategic effort to build relationships. You want them to be deeper versus a wide array of relationships. The agent that can get face to face and get involved with a hyper local focus is going to win.

4. How do you serve agents?

Our company does monthly mailed newsletters that will change your business. It will help you change your business. It will assist you in converting prospects to clients to referrals. Do you want 10,000 Facebook fans? We can help you with that.

Final Thoughts:

By building deep relationships you have the ability to build a strong business that you enjoy. You need to take the time to consider where you want to go and how to get there.

Part Two: The Truth

The truth about a career in real estate is simultaneously simple and complex.

THE SIMPLE TRUTH

The simplest way I know to think about a career in residential real estate sales is this:

You are building a business to represent clients in a large transaction. You'll need to do that well. You'll need to generate a consistent flow of clients and potential clients. You'll need to generate enough revenue to cover your fixed and variable costs plus a reasonable profit to pay yourself.

This is how successful businesses work.

You'll need to recognize the obvious and not-so-obvious differences in service and product-based businesses, independent contractor and employee situations, commission and salary income, technical and emotional communication, and at minimum, have a high tolerance for uncertainty and inconsistency.

Granted, you can abandon these ideas and wing it. Some have succeeded with that approach, but very, very few. Those that took a haphazard route to real estate success leave no clues for the rest of us to repeat or model. That, my friends, would be pure foolishness.

I train my team and my coaching / consulting clients on twelve simple steps to, "Old School ,- Money Making, - People Serving, - Real Estate "'strategies"' that are not rocket science, but are simple and effective for building the sustainable, predictable, repeatable success in real estate sales that so many of us are after.

Implement these at your own benefit:

1. Talk to a lot of people.
One of the absolute most basic elements of a successful residential real estate career is building a large network of relationships with people who know you, like you and trust you. This is an easy and very natural idea to partially implement for most outgoing and stereotypical sales people. However, to fully implement this idea, you must focus more on the people who don't yet know you, like you or trust you. A simple and easy to implement way of looking at this involves creating an exhaustive list of all your existing relationships. Then, divide that list into three groups. The first list will be the people who know you but may not know you well enough to like you beyond an acquaintance level and certainly don't have a high level of trust in you yet. The second list is for people who know you a bit better and clearly like you but most likely don't have any level of trust for you beyond the casual friend or friend-of-a-friend level. The third list is for the people who know you, like you and trust you and who have made that clear to you.

Now, your goal is to move people from the first list to the second list and from the second list to the third over time.

But, the most overlooked part of the entire process is getting more and more people on the first list. This requires good old-fashioned effort. Start by simply talking to a lot of people.

BONUS

Link to METS video:
5LiesBook.com/Resources

Tomorrow is National Hug Your Favorite Realtor Day.

So if we don't cross paths you can just send me a referral.

LighterSide
OF REAL ESTATE

2. **Be freakishly knowledgeable.**
Know your statistics, history, trends, and issues of the day.

While this sounds difficult, it is actually very simple. You need to know more than your ideal client, and you need to be able to make that very clear in a respectful and valuable way. When presented with the opportunity of a seemingly random conversation about "the market" or a specific home or transaction, you should, at a minimum, know some relevant information that you can share. Over the course of my career as an agent, then broker and long-time brokerage owner and team leader, I've found that just a few simple statistics cover almost any situation.

If you'll commit to staying current on your local market's absorption rate, average days on market and average price per square foot at no more than three benchmarks, you'll be and come across as a fantastically knowledgeable real estate professional.

In the spirit of keeping it simple, here is a very basic break down of those three statistics and how to use them.

Absorption rate: Absorption rate is the same as months of inventory, an estimate of how fast listings are currently selling measured in months. For example, if 100 properties sell per month and there are 800 properties for sale - there is an eight-month supply of inventory before counting the additional properties that will come on the market. I teach my team and my coaching and consulting clients that a normal market has four-to-six months of inventory or an absorption rate of 4.0 – 6.0.

If the absorption rate is less than 4.0, you are in a "seller's market," where sellers have more leverage in negotiations with buyers because buyers have fewer homes to choose from.

If the absorption rate is greater than 6.0 you are experiencing a "buyer's market," where buyers have more leverage in negations with sellers because buyers have plenty of homes to choose from.

Average Days on Market: Average days on market is a self-explanatory statistic. It calculates how long homes are taking to sell. What it doesn't calculate are the endless number of factors that cause a property to sell fast or slow. Simply stated, you want to know the average number of days it is currently taking to sell homes in at least the three most common price ranges in your key geographic focus areas. It wouldn't hurt to have a ballpark idea of the differences in days on market (DOM) between varying types of properties as well.

Average Price Per Square Foot: Average price per square foot is a key statistic to have on hand at all times. You'll miss frequent opportunities to position yourself as an expert and to earn business if you can't provide at least an educated range for a property value when asked in passing.

I recommend that you stay current with the average price per foot of homes in your key areas of focus at the top, middle and bottom of the price range. Again, it would benefit you to know those numbers for different property types as well.

Most multiple listing systems produce these statistics regularly and many companies provide attractively formatted reports that you can study as well as share with clients and potential clients.

In addition to statistics, you should read and pay attention to local, regional and national news about relevant information. Tax law changes, local development, employment trends and politics all have real impact on homeowners and you'll either be a leading voice who can interpret that for the use of local homeowners or not. You get to choose!

BONUS

Link to Example Real Market Report:
5LiesBook.com/Resources

Dear Clients,
I love you more than coffee,
just not before coffee.

LighterSide

3. Think Long-Term.

Don't be stupid. It ain't gonna happen overnight. More people buy books, watch webinars and click on ads with outrageous headlines about million dollar first years and 1,000 percent annual growth than those that offer exciting, but achievable, repeatable and healthy approaches to a real estate career.

By all means, read books, watch webinars and look at options to invest in your business, but don't be intoxicated with the smoke and mirrors of instant success. The good news is that simple, smart, disciplined long-term thinking can and occasionally does lead to quick growth. That quick growth is more sustainable when achieved with the end, and I mean way down the road end, in mind.

Rapid growth built with a "now, now, now" mentality rarely, if ever, leads to a long, meaningful career.

Put in the time in the beginning to master the basics. Set attainable goals that excite you but recognize that you are not a master yet. Respect this business enough to know that you can't be a teacher before you are a student and you can't deliver world class value before you deliver the basics.

When making commitments, setting goals and/or writing a business plan, start with a long-term ten-plus-year vision of where you'd like to be as a person, family member, friend etc. and then work backwards. Create a five-year vision, then a three-year and only after all of that is complete and abundantly clear in your mind and on paper or a computer screen, craft a plan for your next year.

After that, narrow your commitment or plan (I prefer commitment) to a 90-day version and chunk out the topics you need to study, skills you need to practice, strategies you need to test and get to work.

Nope, stop adding to it. Just get to work.

BONUS

Link to Planning Documents:
5LiesBook.com/Resources

4.Think clients first, company or team second and self-last.

How many people are looking out for your income? Is it just you? I don't think that's wise for someone in an industry spread so thin with countless ways to waste money, time, influence, energy and focus.

I suggest you build a virtually indestructible fortress of support from absolutely thrilled clients, forever-loyal peers and a personal drive to never ever, ever quit.

It sounds cheesy to literally put your clients' needs ahead of your own. It isn't. Even long after a sale has been made and a commission has been earned, paid, deposited and spent, your client's legitimate needs and your desire to serve them at the highest possible level are your greatest opportunity for success.

It sounds flat out backwards to many to put your brokerage, team or group's needs ahead of your own. It isn't. "I take care of number one," is one of the loneliest, most foolish comments I hear, and I sadly hear it a lot.

When you commit to serving your clients first, your team second and yourself third, you create a compounding benefit for all involved. Change perspectives for a second. Think from the viewpoint of Paul on your team or at your brokerage.

If Paul follows this model, he delivers world-class value to his clients under the same logo and company name as you. That adds value to the shared brand or image that you both use to build your career. This is a good thing.

If Paul puts the team ahead of himself, he's thinking about how his actions and plans will benefit you. If you are part of a great organization, company or team, Paul is not alone. Maria, Jeff, Carl and many others are also looking out for the team. They are all looking out for you. Each of the members of the team has all the members of the team looking out for them, their clients, their income and their desired life.

Do that.

5.Think local / niche.

The first time I heard a speaker say, "get rich in your niche," I assuredly rolled my eyes. I assure you now though that this eye roll was done out of ignorance and pride. Going deep in focus on one area, property type or client type is by far the more profitable and sustainable approach to business. Remaining wide in your focus in hopes of a broader reach and more captured opportunity is one of the most inefficient and costly, not to mention difficult, approaches to small business that exists. Be known for something specific and positive by the exact people you want to be known by. Be a big fish in a small, but plenty big enough pond.

Consider specializing in marketing for sellers of homes on private golf courses or buyers of homes above the mid-level price for your area with swimming pools. Focusing on a very specific niche does not mean that you can never work outside of your niche but not focusing at all will virtually guarantee that you'll never be known as the best or the only great option for a specific segment of the market.

Your goal should be to own that position in the mind of your ideal client. Let's say, for example, that my team and I have an area of specialization around homes on one-to-five acres. (We actually do by the way.)

When my ideal client has the thought, "I think it is time to sell the house and find a bigger house on more land" I want him or her to immediately follow that thought with this one; "I know that Todd Tramonte guy specializes in homes on one to five acres. I'll call him."

This wonderful and exquisitely targeted seller and buyer client would only have that thought if he or she had heard my radio ads, seen my billboard, seen my internet ads, read my direct mail, seen our box truck or repeatedly come across my very specific messaging telling him or her that my team and I specialize in selling homes on one-to-five acres.

Imagine now that this seller also calls Bob from XYZ realty who sent him a postcard or sold a home nearby. Bob is a good guy, he sells a decent number of homes, but his messaging says that he operates with the highest level of ethics and has been in the business for twenty-eight years. Do you think Bob's marketing plan, or lack thereof, will be able to compete with my preemptive marketing that already has me top of mind for this client as the go-to specialist for properties just like his or hers? How about that plus the online, printed and initial consultation information I share with the seller before, during and after our time together? I'm going to win that opportunity every time.

BONUS

Link to Niche Questionnaire:
5LiesBook.com/Resources

6. Obey the law, maintain the standards, be proud to do the right thing.

Do you like sleep? I do. I want to encourage you to do a few things and avoid a few things in order to sleep well at night.

1. Obey the law. <u>All</u> the laws.
2. Tell the truth. Always.
3. Keep your word.
4. Do the right thing, even when it hurts.
5. Be proud but not obnoxious about refusing to compromise on 1-4 above.

No amount of money, ranking, prestige or market share will compensate you for the lost respect, from yourself and others once you go down the path of the shady real estate agent.

<u>Never ever:</u>

1. Deliberately keep information that is required to be disclosed about a defect or imperfection in a home from any party to a transaction.

2. Avoid difficult conversations with clients, agents, lenders, title companies etc. Be the person who finds the solution, not the one who waits for someone else to fix things.

3. Promise a result to a client or transaction partner that you don't have complete confidence you can deliver.

These are common sense for most people, but in the thick of negotiations and the complexity of transactions, these values can get lost.

BONUS

Printable Values Sheet:
5LiesBook.com/Resources

You are immensely capable, so ***choose*** your desired results.
Success is contagious, so put in the work.
Build ***relationships*** you will be proud *to tell your grandchildren* about.
FIGHT THE URGE TO BLEND IN, fall in or phone it in.
Differentiate with EXCELLENCE.
Be more informed, experienced and generous today than you were yesterday and more tomorrow than today. Never stop learning.
Practice like a champion. Root out *negativity* and cast out *doubt*.
Share your gifts and seek out others to compensate for your ever diminishing shortcomings. VISION LEAKS.
Know your purpose in life, remind yourself of it ***daily*** and be **willing to die for it.**
You are the product of your expectations.

The Todd Tramonte Home Selling Team Game Plan for Success -- For as he thinks within himself, so he is. Proverbs 23:7

7. Value time over money.

The absolute most limited resource we have is our time. As difficult as it may seem at times, we at least have the potential to make more money, get more food, meet new people, etc. There is not the slightest opportunity to create more time. While "Back To the Future" was an incredible movie, it isn't real. Sorry folks, no time travel.

I'll make a rare literary reference here and share one of my favorite pieces of symbolism with you.

In nearly every version of Peter Pan, one of the main themes is the refusal to acknowledge time and aging. Tick-Tock Croc, however constantly pursues Captain Hook, the only main character who acknowledges his adulthood. With a ticking alarm clock in his belly, the constant pursuit of a dangerous and hungry animal who literally ticks away every second symbolizes the very real limits of time.

Let's get back to real estate.

You must value time over money. You must budget and allocate your time first. I consistently remind those I lead, coach and train that the best piece of technology we have in our industry is a calendar. Yes, a calendar. You must learn to identify the amount of time you are most productive working without interruption. You must also identify the times of day you are most effective at being responsive to transactional details and client needs. You may find that you work best in ninety-minute blocks with short fifteen-minute breaks in the early part of the day and that you are best at returning calls, writing emails and running errands in the middle part of the afternoon. I'll predict right here that you will not find a better part of the day for prospecting, training and planning than early in the morning. It is the part of the day with the least demands from others. Count on that.

That moment when you leave for vacation....

as a REALTOR®

8. Hard work is required.

Learn to love hard work. The feeling of putting in a full day, week or month for that matter is tremendously rewarding when the work was the right work. There are no short cuts to meaningful success.

One of my long-time coaches always talks about seeking out short term pain. The idea is that short term pain leads to long term gain. This is true in the gym, with your diet, in sales, and in just about every area of life. The opposite is also true. Pursuing short term gain almost always leads to long term pain. Get rich quick schemes lead to staying broke longer. Not going to the gym leads to being unhealthy longer. Eating the delicious sugar leads to less personal health. In our world of residential real estate, putting in the boring, mundane, routine, daily work may look like pain in the short term, but it will lead to long term gain in the way of client relationships, commissions, great team members, systems and on and on.

Cheap wins and short-term victories can come easily on occasion, but sustainable, predictable and consistent income and career happiness come from good old-fashioned hard work. This is true every single time.

Don't buy the lie that you can work smart instead of working hard. You must do both. Now, there is good news with all this work. We work in real estate, and most likely not the part where people swing hammers and lay shingles in 100-degree heat. We have the privilege, yes, it is a privilege, to sit in the air conditioning of our office or car and talk to people who want what we have to offer and are grateful to get it. We get to talk to neighbors, advocate for friends and add value into the lives of new families in our communities. This is not back-breaking work, this is exciting, challenging and meaningful work. This brings me directly to point number nine.

BONUS

View Hustle Video:
5LiesBook.com/Resources

> There was an old woman who lived in a shoe, thanks to a top-performing Realtor who was able to meet her unusual and eccentric needs.
>
> LighterSide OF REAL ESTATE

9. Be thankful.

You are not entitled to anything. Society owes you not one single thing. I believe in the deepest part of my heart and mind that men and women ought to serve each other before we serve ourselves, but I believe that because of my faith in Jesus, who loved me when I was a filthy sinner fully rejecting his love. Outside of individual faith, values or conviction, the community owes you nothing. Be thankful for this opportunity. Be thankful for every potential client. Be thankful for every single referral whether it converts to a sale and a commission or not. Be thankful for hard working and competent transaction partners. Be thankful for the ability to do this work.

When I was in high school I had the privilege of working for my father. It really was a privilege. There were days I certainly wished I worked for a stranger that might hold me to a normal hourly warehouse type standard, but today it is clear that this was a gift. My dear old dad was a learn by doing guy and would throw my brother and me right into a job and let us figure it out. These situations were the seeds of entrepreneurship that I didn't know were being planted in me and I'm not sure he fully understood either. I know he wasn't blind to it though.

My dad also believed in having an absolutely terrible job. So, he arranged at one point for me to work at a car dealership not far from our house. I'll never forget the horrible thought that came to my mind when the manager handed me a black t-shirt as my "uniform" for working outside in the summer heat in Houston, Texas. I hated that job for quite a while, but my dad hounded me with his reason for doing it. He said that I'd always be thankful for my education and for my future jobs because I had had a truly cruddy one. He knew that without having a reference point for a hard, brutally hot job that you basically hate, you may never be grateful for the good stuff.

I'm grateful for the good stuff.

Let me make one somewhat counterintuitive point here though. Be careful, as a true professional, to communicate your gratitude for a client's trust in you with a tone that sends the message that you have been given a gift. I know that may sound strange, but the point I intend to make is this: You should be grateful that a client chose to trust you. You should also be firm and intentional about the fact that you are such a true professional offering such tremendous value that deep down, they should be thanking you for the opportunity to work with you. Your "thank you" should communicate a mutual respect.

BONUS

Link to Gratitude Sheet:
5LiesBook.com/Resources

10. Communicate directly.

Follow this pattern to rank the quality of typical communications:

Face-to-face > phone calls > text > emails > social media > nothing.

There is no more valuable communication between two people than a face-to-face discussion. The next best and most common form of communication in the residential real estate industry is a phone call. Avoid swapping voicemails with important information. Use a voicemail to identify an ideal time to reconnect for a live call so you can address important issues and terms at that point.

Text messages can be highly effective for initial contacts and prospecting but are a poor substitute for a live phone call when it comes time for meaningful dialogue. Never text when you could call if the communication will change anything of significance. Text directions, call to negotiate.

Email is the most overvalued form of communication. It is too easy to send an email when a live conversation would have easily avoided the potential for misunderstood tone, accidental replies to all and many other blunders. Show that you care and pick up the phone. A great use of email is to send documents, and another is to create a note or a record of a recent phone conversation so that it can be revisited and serve as a date and timestamp for the discussion.

Social media is not without merit in professional communication. It is somewhat shocking that this is now a reality, but it is. However, even a direct message through social media is exponentially more likely to be misunderstood or missed altogether than a live meeting or phone call. Much like texting, social media communications are fine for long-term relationship nurturing or for initial contact but are a terrible form of communication for substantive back-and-forth. Pick up the phone.

BONUS

Link to Michael Maher & Levels of Communication: 5LiesBook.com/Resources

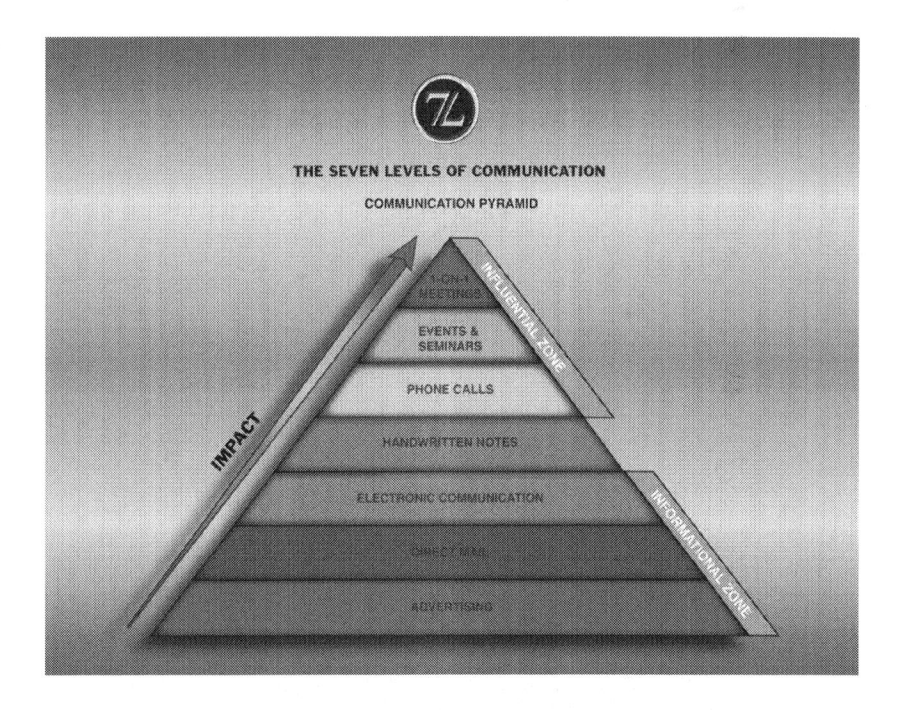

Credit: Michael Maher, "7 Levels of Communication"

11. Shake the trees.

My father is a big fan of the movie Cool Hand Luke. Growing up I worked in his warehouse and sat in on meetings with his salesmen. He sold toner cartridges before it was cool. He used to teach us to get out of the office, get out of our comfort zone and to stir up business with a great Cool Hand Luke quote.

In the movie Luke is a prisoner. The prison guards have a system for letting the prisoners go to the bathroom while out on work crews on the roads. They would let a prisoner go behind a bush as long as they kept shaking the tree to indicate that they were still there and had not tried to escape.

My dad used that scene to tell us to "shake the trees" meaning to be out in the market place to be seen and to make sure that clients and competitors knew we were still there.

Luke does escape by tying a string to the tree and shaking it continuously as he runs away, but I recommend you stay and have an amazing career.

BONUS

List of ways to shake the trees:
5LiesBook.com/Resources

12. Ask for business.

I read in a book a long time ago that you will never G-E-T if you do not A-S-K. This has proven true in my life many times. Friends of mine think I have some secret natural ability to get folks to let me in places I'm not supposed to be or to get special treatment at times. I'd chalk those "advantages" up to simply asking. I ask sales people if that is the best deal they can offer and often get a better deal. I ask hosts and hostesses if I can get a special table at a restaurant, and I've asked travel agents and hotel booking agents for the best rooms or reservations they know of. People usually like to give. It is a wonderful little secret that if you ask for what you want, you've got a much better shot at actually getting it. This is not just a literal statement either. Without going into exhaustive detail here, it is a biblical principle of prayer and a reliable principle of self-motivation too. Let me be clear that I'm not a believer in the prosperity gospel that some teach saying that if you are good and ask God or the universe for a Ferrari, you'll get one. That's definitively bogus.

I do believe that if you pray faithfully, God will give you what you need. The good news is he knows what we need better than we do.

I also believe that if you ask a lot of yourself, you'll tend to deliver. That's a good thing.

BONUS

Scripts for asking for business:
5LiesBook.com/Resources

Expert Interview: Blaise Timco

Founder, SchoolEstate.Com

School Estate is one of the largest Real Estate Schools in Texas with over 75,000 graduating agents. Blaise works as an instructor as well as working closely with the Texas Real Estate Commission.

1. What do you think is the biggest lie you hear or see shared with new agents about real estate?

Agents will tell newcomers this is awesome and fantastic career without sharing the reality of real estate. The other thing I hear real estate agents tell newcomers is this is horrible career do not get into this business. Two very different perspectives but the reality is business does not "just appear" from family and friends. It will take hard work to build your business.

2. What is the best advice you have about building a real estate career?

People often look for a magic wand to make them successful. There is not one magic solution. You must wake up daily and work hard. Do the basics: be knowledgeable about real estate, honor your commitments and build relationships with people.

3. What is the best long-term truth you have learned?

Keep learning and be extremely knowledgeable about the market in general. Be especially knowledgeable in the neighborhoods where you focus. People pay for expertise and confidence. Plug into the area you want to focus on, so you can become the go to person for that niche.

4. How do you serve agents?

School Estate has industry leaders who are teachers write curriculum that will prepare agents to get their license. We are unique in that we help students understand they are a business owner not just a license holder. We help new agents get a jump start on their business.

Final Thoughts:

Keep working on and in your business. Learning to be the expert with your continuing education and seeking out mentors can help propel you to success.

THE COMPLEX TRUTH

Knowing that there are at least five very dangerous lies that the world tells people about a career in residential real estate and having read 12 simple truths about how to be successful, here are just a few ways that adding a bit of complexity to your business at the appropriate time (after you've mastered many of the simpler strategies) can be transformational in your career.

Marketing

First, you must decide who has a problem that needs to be solved or a desire that needs to be met in the marketplace. This helps you define your market. Most real estate agents think about a geographic area when they read the word market but focus on the group of people with whom you intend to work. Define which group has a need that you can serve.

Second, you'll need to craft a specific message that speaks directly to that ideal market of people you just defined. The best copywriters, marketers and advertisers on earth call this "entering the conversation that is already happening in their mind." Speak directly to the challenges or goals that they are repeating to themselves as they go throughout their day. Do not write a headline or tag line that sounds cool to you, write one that causes your ideal client to think "Finally, this is exactly what I need."

Third, you will carefully select the best media (one-to-three) to deliver that exact message to that exact market. Let's say your ideal market is empty nesters living in high-end homes on land, and they want to downsize and reduce maintenance. Your ideal message is "Your acreage property sold, and your life simplified in 60 days or less guaranteed." Now you must determine where that market wants to consume that message. Do empty nesters most likely read the newspaper, social media or direct mail pieces? Do they listen to AM radio or FM radio? Do they open envelope mail or look at postcards? Would they use a company that sponsored a local team? The media you use to deliver the message must match the market.

That's the correct order:

First you must define the market. Only then do you craft your message. The last thing is to choose the correct one-to-three media to deliver the message in the most effective way to the market.

Somewhere north of 75% of all marketers get this out of order. You are now a business owner and business owners must at least consider utilizing smart marketing.

The vast majority of business owners rushes past this and choose either the message or the media first with no consideration for whether or not there is a viable market. They have something they want to say or do. They think

TV commercials are cool. They saw another guy apparently hitting it big with post cards.

However, until all three pieces of the puzzle are put together to create a well-designed picture of your business growth, you'll be spinning your wheels at best and wasting time and most likely money for sure.

Be aware that your media may be word of mouth. A little complexity in your business doesn't have to look like an advanced math calculation. Simple and complex do go together, but simple and lazy or simple and foolish do not work out well.

Excellence

Now that you have added some sophisticated but still simple ideas to your business and created real clarity around who you want to work with, how you will help them and how you'll tell them what you can do, you need to back that offer or promise up with expertise.

Never, ever stop learning. A complex training plan with a desire for maintaining simplicity just looks like thinking ahead. When you build out your schedule to prioritize time over money, you'll commit to growing in some way each day. Read a relevant book for 30 minutes each day. Listen to an industry or related podcast for 30 minutes. Watch a free educational video or webinar. Role play with an agent in your office or by phone from anywhere in the world three times per week. Listen to audio recordings of scripts in the car or on a jog. Attend at least one industry or related conference each year.

Being coached is a must. The world's most elite performers whether it be athletes, actors, or CEOs have coaches, consultants and boards of advisors that regularly challenge them to grow, resource them to stretch their capabilities, and provide accountability or competition to fuel their aspirations.

You simply must have a coach. This can be paid coaching or a willing mentor. Both are excellent. Having neither is not an option if you plan to be a high performer. You will not reach a point of master and remain there for long if you fail to continue to grow and learn.

I've seen many people credited with the following quote, but regardless of who said or wrote it, it remains true.

Success is not owned, it is rented...and the rent is due every day.

This business changes constantly. The laws, regulations, seasons, lending impact, economic climate, political climate, license requirements, national, regional, and local -job markets, consumer confidence and on and on and on change. It is always changing. You must change too. Change for the better.

Around our office at the Todd Tramonte Home Selling Team, we strive to "Differentiate with excellence!"

Purpose

One of the hardest things for Americans to discern is our own motivation, our reason why or our purpose. This, to me, is a great irony. We have more opportunity, freedom and peace than any country in the world. We have a culture built on independence, building things, creating our future and providing abundance. Yet, we are simultaneously so spoiled with it all that we forget, often for years at a time, what we want.

We have so much material possession that it clouds our thinking about our most real desires. We're presented with so many viable options for our future that it can be tremendously difficult to focus on one that matters, brings us joy and fulfills a natural giftedness and instinct. Were we in more desperate situations, our single focus may simply be survival or basic provision for our families. If you do find yourself in one of those situations, we live in a wonderful country where many are eager to help.

So, what is your purpose? What is your deepest reason for wanting to succeed in residential real estate sales or leadership? Do you know? Do you know why you want to take on the lies the culture tells? Do you know what drives you to be one of the rare few who succeed at a full-time, full income level? Are you clear on your natural gifts and the things that make you feel alive? There are many great profiles you can take, books you can read and people you can talk with to discover this.

Discover this first. Discover these crucial truths before you build a life and a business on the wrong ones... the lies.

Expert Interview: Mike Bell

Founder – The Lighter Side of Real Estate

Mike Bell is a former real estate agent, former appraiser, and former failure at social media... that is, until he discovered the concept of "info-tainment." He's now committed to helping real estate agents grow their brand awareness through clever content marketing, both online and offline.

1. What do you think is the biggest lie you hear or see shared with new agents about real estate?

That agents get paid tons of money for doing very little. This is due to a general misperception about what agents actually do and how they get compensated (including all the expenses involved).

2. What is the best advice you have for building a real estate career?

To be successful in real estate, you need three bones: A wishbone, a backbone, and funny bone.

3. What is the best long-term truth you have learned?

Real estate, and business in general, is a marathon not a sprint. Sometimes you must forfeit short-term gains to produce long-term wins.

4. How do you serve agents?

As founder of the Lighter Side of Real Estate, I use humor to provide agents with an escape from the daily real estate hustle.

Final Thoughts

The real estate industry can be heavy at times. Stressful, too. And competitive. We all know this. But if you're not laughing, you're not living. To learn more about Mike Bell's services, go to: https://innercircle.lightersideofrealestate.com/join-innercircle

An Amazing FREE Offer for You!

For trusting me with your time to read this book, I'd like to offer you FREE access to one of my private coaching groups. Jump in at no charge and stay in long term only if you love it. Join agents from all over North America, as well as my team, as we sharpen our skills, improve our strategy, and share our wins each week.

Visit:

www.ToddsCoaching.com

and choose Members Only Business Builders Group to grab your spot now. Use promo code FREE60 to get 60 days of weekly group calls and private Facebook group access at no charge!

I'm confident that you'll find it worth your time to sign up and make use of the training provided. When I was a new agent I never had a mentor outside of the books I read, tapes I listened to and seminars I attended. As I started to have success, I began to reinvest my profits into learning from some of the best business minds from inside and outside of the real estate community.

What I share with my consulting and coaching clients are the brutally honest lessons I've learned as well as the cool shiny stuff I've created myself. I believe in providing value way beyond the expectation of my clients, so I'm giving you a free 60-day trial of our Members Only Business

Builders group to help you implement some of my ideas or adopt my way of thinking.

If you don't get at least $1,000 of value and ideas from the membership, just let me know and I'll send you a box with three of my favorite books from other real estate leaders. It's FREE, so go sign up now at:

www.ToddsCoaching.com

then, shoot me an email at REGS@ToddTramonte.com and let me know how you like the book.

To your dreams and mine,

Todd Tramonte

APPENDIX

Feedback from "Real" Real Estate Agents

Robert – Real Estate Agent, Four Years' Experience

1. What tip was a big take away for new agents?

Learning to see past the split that a broker can give you and measure the real lifetime value of a broker's contribution to your business is a huge first step in building a successful business. Choosing based on a split is downright ignorant and lazy. Your bottom line will not benefit from a higher split if your broker cannot help you to bring in new business or close a deal.

2. Which of the lies jumps out at you?

Lie number three - great part time opportunity.

I initially pursued my license as a means of supplementing my income when I was an employee for a non-profit. Todd shared his wisdom for folks looking to "do real estate" part-time. His advice: "Don't." He elaborated by explaining that it's a complete disservice to my clients, who are likely limited to close (and naive) friends if I'm only doing it part time. To claim I am their best option to help them navigate such a life-changing decision when I'm not devoting consistent time to my craft is ignorant at best and downright selfish at worst. You can't keep up if you're not all in. It takes a full-time professional to navigate the intricacies and complexities of a transaction and do so in a manner that leads the client to their best possible outcome. Leading a transaction takes a high degree of knowledge and intuition to bring understanding and peace to a complex and emotional process. The measure of an agent's worth is not just that they got to the closing table, but how they added value to their client en route to the closing table. I don't believe part-time agents can add the same degree of value as committed, full-time professional agents. As time goes on, the truth of his answer continues to ring true. Needless to say, I never worked a single deal as a part-time agent.

3. What are the benefits of learning these lies up front?

Learning right the first time is significantly easier than trying to undo bad habits and destructive patterns. Failure to grasp the basics of building a pipeline, converting opportunity and serving clients will keep you from ever getting out of the "up front" stage of a career in real estate. It's do or die. Furthermore, taking the time to make an up-front investment in your career will position you to win against the majority of agents who have been around longer but never put forth the effort to refine their craft and become an expert in the industry.

Kristin – Real Estate Agent, Three Years' Experience

1. What tip was a big take away for new agents?

I would say the entire book was helpful. When I first started, it was a trend that people joined to have flexibility with their career. But that's what killed me – I had no structure. I wanted and needed structure, but no one would teach me. It was always, "find out what works for you. I was ALWAYS told by other brokers to work my sphere of influence to build a business, but I had just moved to the area and didn't know anyone. The response to building a sphere of influence was to go join an organization I was interested in and volunteer.

2. Which of the lies jumps out at you?

Definitely lie number four - The bigger the split, the better the broker. The bigger the split, the more you are getting ripped off. What I found is that with the right broker I got so much more in training, mentorship, learning, etc.

3. What are the benefits of learning these lies up front?

If I had had this information when I started my real estate career, I could have saved a lot of time and frustration, as well as made significantly more money. While advancing in your career, you should expect to train and study for a long time to be an expert, and a career in real estate is no exception. To be of value to your clients, you need to know the market, know the laws and be skilled in negotiation. This book reminds me that you need to be with a broker that supports you and helps you get to that level of expertise because people will pay for expertise. At the beginning of my career I did not realize this, and it took me much longer to be successful.

Leah – Real Estate Agent, Four Months Experience

1. What tip was a big take away for new agents?

Be freakishly knowledgeable. There are tons of so called real estate professionals out there. You need to set yourself apart by your expertise and your professionalism.

2. Which of the lies jumps out at you?

Lie Number Three - Real Estate isn't a part time gig if you want to offer world class value to your clients. You must have structure in your daily schedule, not just work your sphere and work with a great broker who is going to push you and help you grow daily. This is a full-time job and not just something that can or should be done on the side (if you want to do it correctly, that is).

3. What are the benefits of learning these lies up front?

While learning on the fly can be a great way to learn – it is NOT cool to learn at the expense of your clients with their largest financial purchase. Your clients will be able to tell if this is your first transaction by the way you carry yourself and how knowledgeable you are throughout the process.

John – Real Estate Agent, Six Years' Experience

1. What tip was a big take away for new agents?

Great overview and a comprehensive view of what you need to do to get started and run your real estate business. Todd doesn't mince words when he tells you you will have to work hard.

2. Which of the lies jumps out at you?

Lie Number 1 – You will have complete flexibility with your time.

You must be disciplined. You can structure your time to accommodate your personal needs, but you must have structure to prospect, meet with your clients and do the things that will make you successful.

3. What are the benefits of learning these lies up front?

Learning upfront means you can avoid a lot of unnecessary trial, error and pain.

Jeremy – Real Estate Agent, Eight Months Experience

1. What tip was a big take away for new agents?

A successful career in real estate is so much different than the mainstream media portrays it as (shocking!). It truly takes discipline and a well-thought-out game plan to enjoy a successful career and the flexibility that draws so many new agents to the industry.

2. Which of the lies jumps out at you?

It was actually Simple Truth #3 that spoke most to me. I quickly found that thinking long term is vital for a new agent's success. It is almost inevitable to sign your first client or two and then spend all your time focusing on closing a deal instead of continuing to not only train daily, but to continue building your pipeline. Thanks to the ideas found in this book, I caught this bad habit early and learned to think long term and continue building my business daily.

3. What are the benefits of learning these lies up front?

Recognizing these lies as a new agent keeps you from setting unrealistic expectations based on what the world tells you is the "standard". Unmet expectations are crippling and are often the reason agents do not succeed in this industry. Beginning a real estate career knowing these lies will allow you to set realistic goals and have a real vision for what can be accomplished with proper training and discipline.

David – Real Estate Agent, Three Years' Experience

1. What tip was a big take away for new agents?

Hard work is required. You have to handle multiple tasks. There is a lot of variety which can be fun, but you will need to put in the work to get results. You may get small wins but if you are going to be successful you need to "shake the trees."

2. Which of the lies jumps out at you?

Lie number three is the biggest. If you want to be successful and serve your clients well, you will be all in. There is no way to do that part time. It takes time and you must be available.

3. What are the benefits of learning these lies up front?

My perception was that this would be easy. My friends and family would call me, and I would sell a lot of houses. As a gregarious, good person that they would want to do business with me. If I had had this book and a more realistic sense of what was required I could have ramped up faster.

Megan – Real Estate Agent, Two Years' Experience

1. What tip was a big take away for new agents?

You need strong communication skills and to work on building relationships to have a successful real estate business. Yes, you need to be great at the technical aspects of real estate, but you need to care for your clients at a personal level to be excellent.

2. Which of the lies jumps out at you?

Lie number three- this is not a part time job – you don't want a part time lawyer or a part time CPA nor do you want a part time real estate agent. You need to do this full time not in addition to something else to be successful. I had originally planned to do real estate on the side of my full-time job. This book cements the idea that you will never build your business if you don't work at it full time.

3. What are the benefits of learning these lies up front?

You will be properly prepared that this is a career that requires you to have excellent organizational skills. You will need to be motivated. The business will not come to you – you will have to hustle to gain clients.

Clarissa – Real Estate Agent, Six Months Experience

1. What tip was a big take away for new agents?

Real Estate is not a part time career. I honestly don't believe the words part time and career should even go together. To be successful in real estate there is no other way to go than full time. Now that I am a full-time agent I feel like there is not enough time in the day. I can fill every hour of the day every day of the week.

2. Which of the lies jumps out at you?

Value time over money - you can't get time back. By implementing the use of a calendar and schedule, my time throughout the day is used appropriately.

3. What are the benefits of learning these lies up front?

Learning up front has been so valuable. Being a new agent myself and having other friends who have just started in the industry, I have seen firsthand how important it is to be trained. Developing my knowledge in how to better communicate with and treat my clients has been the biggest take away.

NOTES:

Made in the USA
Middletown, DE
19 November 2018